GRIMSBY DOCKS

Other Books by Ian Gouge

Novels and Novellas

17 Alma Road - Coverstory books, 2024
Tilt - Coverstory books, 2023
Once Significant Others - Coverstory books, 2023
On Parliament Hill - Coverstory books, 2021
A Pattern of Sorts - Coverstory books, 2020
The Opposite of Remembering - Coverstory books, 2020
At Maunston Quay - Coverstory books, 2019
An Infinity of Mirrors - Coverstory books, 2018 (2nd ed.)
The Big Frog Theory - Coverstory books, 2018 (2nd ed.)
Losing Moby Dick and Other Stories - Coverstory books, 2017

Short Stories

An Irregular Piece of Sky - Coverstory books, 2023
Degrees of Separation - Coverstory books, 2018
Secrets & Wisdom - Paperback, 2017

Poetry

Crash - Coverstory books, 2023
not the Sonnets - Coverstory books, 2023
Selected Poems: 1976-2022 - Coverstory books, 2022
The Homelessness of a Child - Coverstory books, 2021
The Myths of Native Trees - Coverstory books, 2020
First-time Visions of Earth from Space - Coverstory books, 2019
After the Rehearsals - Coverstory books, 2018
Punctuations from History - Coverstory books, 2018
Human Archaeology - Paperback, 2017
Collected Poems (1979-2016) - KDP, 2017

Non-Fiction

Shrapnel from a Writing Life - Coverstory books, 2022

IAN GOUGE

GRIMSBY DOCKS

First published in hardback format by Coverstory books, 2024

ISBN 978-1-7384693-7-6

Copyright © Ian Gouge 2024

The right of Ian Gouge to be identified as the author of this work has been asserted by them in accordance with the Copyright, Designs and Patents Act 1988.

The cover image is based on a photograph taken by the author © Ian Gouge 2024

All rights reserved.

No part of this publication may be reproduced, circulated, stored in a system from which it can be retrieved, or transmitted in any form without the prior permission of the publisher in writing.

www.iangouge.com

www.coverstorybooks.com

Contents

shell 3
skylights 5
butterflies 7
queues 9
shutters..11
scaffolding...13
hard lines...15
dissolved..17
when is an open door not open 19
boardgame...21
idle chatter 23
keel-hauled..25
exhausted 27
derelict...29
carcass 31
when the roof caved in 33
sensory deprivation 35
ribs...37
(dis)assembly 39
before & after..41
tethered 43
whodunit 45
divorced...47
surf 'n' turf 49
shelter 51

Acknowledgements...53

shell

a snow-white wig is perched
like a feathery fascinator
to distract the eye
from the larger question

is there anything beneath

is its owner still in residence
grimly holding on
expecting
a tide that will never come
not here
on the walkway concrete

I have seen people
create a shell around their hearts
and persuade themselves it is strong
yet all the while fearing it can be crushed
by the heavy boots of disappointment
or betrayal
or the unrequited

skylights

shouts cascade down the concrete steps
pinballing between rafters like
the boom of a foreman
the shrill laughter from nylon-clad gutters
the white-coated shouting the odds
as they barter prices for the day

stairs are thronged like escalators
bodies following ant-like trails
up and down
laden and unladen
compulsively addicted to the hive

through skylights
narrow shafts of light spear down
on puddles and fish scales
then ricochet around the hall
like a shoal of bullets

hours later
the rhythms of stiff brushes
sweeping away a day's waste
the wash-down in readiness for tomorrow's catch

years later
nothing but silence
beams from broken skylights
dying on the floor

butterflies

in summer they bask against the brick
pin themselves to the last vestiges of white
then rise to the roof-top buddleia to feed
or lured through broken windows
seek respite from less clement weather
where predators might perch
camouflaged in funereal feathers

I know nothing of butterflies
other than their addiction to these purple flowers
I know nothing of this building
nor the ghosts that flit inside
only that it   and they   are broken now
recycled as habitat
for buddleia and butterflies

queues

for no obvious reason
even the pigeons appear to queue
keeping their distance as if in line for an ATM
or waiting for the January sales

no echoes of Hitchcock here
this is patience without menace

dodging ropes
metal trugs suspended from girders
previous generations would not have settled thus
disturbed by the yells of the employed
heaving crates on and off trucks

dockers would have queued too
for tea at snap-time
for wages at the week's end
cash-in-hand for a spot of unofficial over-time

and then to trail away post-shift
long straggles of them
heading back to town
the aroma of the sea
soaked into all their surfaces

a quick pint on the way home
before a hot bath
more to camouflage than remove
the narrative of their lives

shutters

do they still go up
the shutters
their KEEP CLEAR superseded by action
trumped by a more pressing imperative

but with you
everything happened in reverse
the shutters came down
red-flagged warnings
scrawled across your countenance
like permanent ink
listing
what would not be happening

loading least of all

I watch a few lorries
rumble these untended streets
and see if I can predict
which of them might stop just here
to load
or otherwise

but then I was never very good
at predicting the future
nor the motion of shutters
their movement
up
or down

scaffolding

this steel grid is a doppelgänger
for a maze
a game where the challenge
is to make it to the top
avoiding the snakes

it looks easy

the proximity of the bars suggest
nothing more needed than a minor stretch
then you realise there are no ladders
the bars are pointing down
with no way to get up
nor avoid the inevitable slide

this was your view of us all
our lives shorn-up to prevent collapse
and you could see nothing but the ground
hurtling towards you as you ricocheted
tearing your skin on joining-clasps
breaking bones when you crashed
from one level to the next

there was no mattress
awaiting the culmination of your fall

later
we laid flowers at the spot where you came to rest
secretly glad our own scaffolding remained intact

hard lines

they sit embedded in concrete
like a broken equals sign
the rot long set-in
all answers now misplaced

encroachment is fractional
almost an after-thought
and where cement has failed to bind
nature has taken root

green punctuates this urban landscape
dull olive in spite of the sun
second-class verdancy resigned
to making do

any port in a storm
you might say

nearby in the café
through a frying-fat fog
a remainder of workers indulge in breakfast
talk of how things were
reminisce about youngsters
hanging from cranes in their underpants

a mobile phone rings
its owner laughs
the wife he says ignoring it
I've already told her I'm busy
doing a bit of business

on his plate two sausages
parallel parked
await the tines of his fork

dissolved

there would have been a point
this year, last year, the year before
when the question was asked
what are we going to do about…

the answer would have tolled like the bell
on a buoy lost in the fret

when did they stop repairing the facade
abandon render-cracks and splintered wood
to raise the white flag

and elsewhere
other walls and doors and windows
have submitted too

as soon as one folded they were all going

those few that remain play second fiddle
to the new marina where gleaming white yachts
are polished and cared for
bob in berths once reserved for trawlers
the mast-slap of ropes a modern backing-track
replacing the old dockers' shouts and songs
long since sucked out to sea
on a tide that will never turn

Notes: Freshney Fish Sales was incorporated on 3rd October 2007 and dissolved on 25th July 2023. At Companies House its trade is listed as "wholesaler of other food, including fish, crustaceans and molluscs". The River Freshney is a river in the English county of North East Lincolnshire. The town of Grimsby stands on its banks. (Wikipedia)

when is an open door not open

like letterboxes
the doors are both open and closed
invitation and denial

you yearn to look inside
seduced by the mythology of secrets
the lure of discovery

yet know you'd find
nothing but the remnants
from furnishings and people

how guarded we are
inclined to offer tell-tale glimpses
thus far no further

my doors are kept shut
since i discovered the immutability
of chains and padlocks

pretence embraced
in a hint that one day i'd let you through
to illuminate the darkness

but now i have lost the key
fallen through a key-shaped pocket-hole
and as the facade crumbles

a question nags
when is an open door not open
and i find its answer is one i've always known

boardgame

reminded of mancala or backgammon
i wonder whose turn it is to move
and who moved last
and whether the rules of the game
are known instinctively
part of the dna
there in the egg
as it were

there is peril in the playing space
some unblanked squares made dangerous by shards of glass

yet i am struck by the birds' nonchalance
the way they perch
just off-centre
and observation shows a move is in progress
bottom left

perhaps it will force a bird to fly away
vanquished by a gambit of some finesse or
if not expelled from the game
compelled to risk the razors in the shards

idle chatter

imagine the conversation
as if they had caught each other
hanging out the washing
compelled to lean on the fence
and chat about neighbours
the state of the world

i remember when this window had glass

and when the frame wasn't broken

inside
other whispers leach through cracked paint
await their chance to fly away

what did you think to the match on saturday

*did you hear about young clive
and that lass from woolworth's*

such questions in that ghostly register
leave the pigeons unflustered
neither the legacy of the past
nor the present decay
their particular concern

keel-hauled

the arc is profoundly elegant
elevating the crudity of metal

yet what once moved smoothly
caressing the hulls of small boats
to be readied for travails at sea
is now set rigid
rust-caked by redundancy

no amount of muscle or grease
can liberate it

not that it matters now

there are no more hulls to cradle
no vessels to protect
the mummified rollers
evidence of a history soon no-one will recall
no-one will have lived

exhausted

the eyes are boarded-up
as if settled for a doze
a constitutional slipped beyond sleep
to the permanently comatose

in the tossing of the wind
pipes grimed and greasy
brickwork stubbled like a chin
trespassed beyond decency

this is a face not for opening
its secrets hidden where they belong
untroubled by idle chatter
the accompaniment of song

the heaters and chillers are silent too
their lungs not tugging at the air
the mothballing embalmers
have long since fled from there

unable to keep pace with dying
it's a body still hoping for the throng
return of the blood-pulse of chatter
and the heartbeat of song

derelict

caved in
open to the elements
mortar that once kept the walls intact
is pale and crumbing
laths and lintels
subject to seasonal attrition

in places light breaks through
glimpses of how things have changed
past life trashed
like a bullied sandcastle

when my friend's partner died
it was like a roof giving way
and now open-mouthed
in a silent scream of confusion
they await the wrecking ball
that will put an end to their misery

carcass

stark against the pale sky
the frame of a Rubik's cube
or the skeleton of a building
all that could be unscrewed
dismantled
removed in some crude act of recycling

detritus litters the foreground
twisted rusting metal
become avant-garde planters
for indiscriminate and unruly weeds
impervious to order

what went on there
what shouts and curses once spilled down
from that now-abandoned box
what trades pursued
what things were taken
and turned one into another
like the cube itself
now gutted
filleted

other than my camera
there's nothing left to gnaw
at the remnants of its carcass

when the roof caved in

who heard the crash when the beams gave way
fractured timbers and an avalanche of slates
falling through a tangle of rusting girders
and long-rotted flooring

perhaps an overnight storm
shattered the camel's spine

do the few who still walk this way to work
look up only to remark

it was just a matter of time
or
well then

shuffling towards the fag-end of their careers
they move on much as i
forced to face facts after life caved in
your leaving me exposing its fragile fabric
buckling as the rain poured through
to warp outdated parquet
swell and jam doors
shatter windows

occasionally i look upon the relic of myself
and pass comment

well then
and
it was only a matter of time

sensory deprivation

presumably they could do what they wanted
beyond the boundaries of yellow lines
and floor-etched periphery

perhaps they took their breaks in timetabled shifts
fag-break
snap-time
perhaps there was an area in which to gob
expel the stale of tobacco
the tannic tang of pg-tips
somewhere to toss the ends of unpalatable baps
a safe space in which to indulge collective venom

the bouquet of fish and fags never left them
no matter what

you can't imagine a sign
powerful enough to stop the cussing
narrow vocabularies of blue
accompanying the marlboros and butties
unfiltered linguistics
walking the taut rope of banter
a hard fall either side

perhaps the sign was a special commission
a précis of management's tablets of stone
perhaps the last of its kind
the one faded memorial in this bleak graveyard
we still find mildly amusing

ribs

beneath the ribs that keep these buildings joined
or chaperoned and far apart
no heart beats
the remnants of a bridge
evidence of a once-struck deal
between partners

perched like pigeons at either end of our sofa
after the dull mechanics of dinner
a couple whose love has also decayed
the bridge between them broken

cross-armed he sits dark and brooding
she cross-legged is happy to flash
some flesh above the knee
speaks cheerily of the future's green shoots

and we
like the ribs between them
listen for a heartbeat
covet what she promises
if only for his sake

(dis)assembly

leave the pitted concrete path
stumble over scrub and unconvincing grass
to discover instruction in repose
way-marker of the past

what could ignite
now the buildings are gone

rather than crudely bulldozed
you want to imagine the pole felled lumberjack-style
ceremoniously downed by dockers
donned in borrowed check shirts just for the craic
singing a monty python song

you assume the sign was snapped in the fall
the 'a' surrendering
no longer needed
yet you are beguiled by the notion
of deliberate fracturing
as if someone was intending
to prefix the message with more appropriate letters

there could be something profound in that
poetic even
and for a moment you allow the reformed image
to settle in your mind
before stepping back to the path
and on to another exhibit of disassembly

before & after

and in-between
wisps of smoke from the wand
that triggered transformation
potteresque

the image is a scrapbook of contradictions
evidence of old and new
the derelict and the pristine
and squashed in a sandwich of blue
reflection blurs both sides of the story
in a smudge of uniformity

grimsby docks
wanted dead and alive

on his forty-footer
Ralph casts a momentary glance to the hulk of the past
remembers feint tales of his uncle Reg
out in all weathers until the storm that claimed him
then he looks to the perfect azure sky
remembers the afternoon's forecast
checks his unblemished nylon ropes
taut in shining chrome pulleys

tethered

it could be a scene from a war movie
you know the story
where one side needs to destroy a bridge
and the other preserve it

kwai or remagen
or a bridge too far

on the water's surface
smithereen shards
haphazard rafts of wood
like a kid's construction game
abandoned in frustration
jenga fallen

one plank remains tethered
not undone by detonation or tide or weather
hope's final vestige clinging on

what is it that still ties us together
so long after you laid the charge
set the timer on the fuse
watched our love go up in smoke

one day soon
i plan to loose the hawser's knot
and set us both free

whodunit

rotted and tinder-dry
a ramshackle pyramid awaits a spark
or a guy fawkes to burn

something else sacrificial
the last rites whispered by crackling flame

then that will be the end of it
incriminating black ash
the final dregs of evidence
blown away by an indifferent wind
dragged by tides and undertow
into the north sea

like disposing of a body
and covering-up the crime

divorced

once sledgehammered into place
what force tore these corroding spikes asunder
leaving brittle sleepers
their wood flaking like sheets of paper
that splinter with the slightest force

work your way to the book's heart
each turned page
encroaching on the story's inevitable denouement

there will be anticlimax
when the iron falls from the wood
to resonate hollow on the concrete below
leaving nothing but a void
the place where two hearts
of young and unseasoned oak
were pressed earnestly together
certain nothing could ever separate them

surf 'n' turf

perhaps the crab put up a fight
before it was hollowed out
the missing claw a crustacean ring-pull
the way in to extract a sweet reward
then
discarded like the twisted pepsi
the shell tossed to the lay-by
where thin strands of grass
compete with pale weeds for meagre existence

it was probably a gull
drilled through the shell
a trucker on the verge of a long haul
who drained the caffeine
both hoping each would be enough
to keep them going for a while

shelter

they erected a steel fence
at the foot of the railway bridge
to make a cul-de-sac buses can no longer run down
nor juggernauts cut-through
to the warehouses
the loading bays

they left the shelter
now abused for booze and fags
the odd sandwich

filling-up and shooting-up

ask the old man who shuffles past the barrier
what he remembers
and he'll tell you the numbers of the buses
and where they went
reminisce about the job he had at young's
remember friends he lost
smile at a lifetime's legends
crafted from the exploits of unfettered youth

and now
point to the shelter and ask him about that

kids today
don't know they're born

then watch as he shuffles away
and into history

Acknowledgements

My heartfelt thanks to Jim Friedman whose close reading of a draft of this collection — and subsequent insightful suggestions — have made the final version of *Grimsby Docks* a more robust and cohesive work.

Early versions of "shell", "shutters", "idle chatter" and "dissolved" first appeared on the Substack site https://www.iangouge.substack.com. You can find a selection of the author's other works at this location.

www.ingramcontent.com/pod-product-compliance
Lightning Source LLC
Chambersburg PA
CBHW040731220426
43209CB00086B/1568